Broken to
Blessed

Patricia Zbranek

Broken to Blessed

Trilogy Christian Publishers
A Wholly Owned Subsidary of Trinity Broadcasting Network
2442 Michelle Drive, Tustin, CA 92780

Manufactured in the United States of America
10 9 8 7 6 5 4 3 2 1
Library of Congress Cataloging-in-Publication Data is available.

ISBN 978-1-68556-719-4
E-ISBN 978-1-68556-720-0

Our journey in life has
a beginning and an end.

—Amanda

We know not what lies in between.

This Is My Journey
through Grief and Sorrow

THIS

IS

MY

Story

THE BEGINNING
December 31, 1995

Two Hearts Together Forever

In loving memory of my husband

Jeffrey Lyndon Zbranek

The love of my life
A loving father to our children
A loving Papaw to our grandchildren
But mostly a faithful servant
to our Lord Jesus Christ

Jeff's Favorite Scripture

Jesus replied, "Very truly I tell you, no one can see the kingdom of God unless they are born again."

—John 3:3 NIV

Jeff's heart's desire was that his family and friends would come to know the same Jesus that he knew and loved.

In his own words, "The only good in me is the Jesus in me."

In Memory of Jeff's Parents

Emil William Zbranek
July 13, 1932 – March 6, 2013

& Ruby Jewel Zbranek
July 20, 1939 – July 11, 2021

Walking Together Forever on the Streets of Gold

In Special Memory of My Sister

Who I have missed growing up with every day.

Debra Ann Sliva

July 3, 1959 – July 16, 1975

For Tony and Hazel

God sets the time when those we love are taken from this earthly home to live above. He binds our eyes; we cannot see, but know we this, she lives in peace, a spirit free. Your grief is sharp, but in a while, think of her joy when Jesus said, "Come in, my child." The prayers you prayed, thy will be done; this day the heavenly chorus sang, "Our Debbie's home!" Reach out your hand; He's standing near to comfort and to wipe away the falling tear.

> With deepest love,
> Evelyn Ussery
> July 16, 1975

All My Love

To my children
Dan'Yelle, Jared, and Joshua

To my son-in-law and daughters-in-laws
Johnathan, Jessica, and Rachel

To my grandchildren
Jaden, Jordis, and Joel

To my parents
Tony (PoPo) and Hazel (MoMo)

To my brothers
Pastor Pat, Tony, and Danny

To my brothers-in-laws
Chris, Brian, and Nathan

To my New Hope Church family and
To my family and friends
*Who has supported me, loved me, prayed with me, or who has just sat
and cried with me during this tremendous loss. I love each and every one
of you and so thankful that you are a part of my life.*

*You don't always have to know what to say or even say anything at all.
More than anything, I just needed your presence.*

A special thanks to the ladies in my Grief Share class.
We prayed, we laughed, we cried. We shared our stories.
We will forever be bonded in a very special way.
"See you in Heaven."

Lisa Moya, Barbara Miller, Nancy Bailey, Mary Martinez,
Kim Marceaux, Dan'Yelle Montague, Patricia Zbranek,
Not Pictured Sarah Calderone

DEDICATION

This book is dedicated to all those who have just begun their journey. Who have suffered the loss of a loved one to COVID, other sicknesses, or an unforeseen accident that has left you with a hole in your heart. Whose faith has been shaken, or to those that feel like life has knocked the wind out of you and that you can barely breathe. I am telling you today, look up! Look toward the heavens and call upon the name of the Lord. He is the one who delivers, He is the one who rescues, and He will be the one who saves in times of trouble.

"...I will never leave you, nor forsake you."

— Hebrews 13:5 (NKJV)

Our Father, Our Grandfather

TABLE OF CONTENTS

THE EULOGIES

These are personal tributes from our children to their father at his memorial service.

I am so proud of each of you, and I know that your dad was proud of you as well. I not only see his handprints on your lives, but I see the handprints of God all over you.

I press on to reach the end of the race and receive the heavenly prize for which God, through Christ Jesus, is calling us.

— Philippians 3:14 (NLT)

Dan'Yelle's Eulogy

A couple of days ago, I overheard my grandma telling my mom, "Trisha, I used to pray that you would find someone who would not only love you but someone who would love Dan'Yelle too."

Jeff was the answer to that prayer.

He's been a part of my life since I was four years old. We weren't blood, but that didn't matter. Anytime he would introduce me to someone, he would say, "This is my daughter." I never told him, but it always made me feel so good when he said that.

When I was younger, especially when I was a teenager... I didn't always make it easy on him, but he hung in there. He prayed for me, and he fought for me as if I was his own. Anytime I had a problem or was struggling with something, he would say, "Dan'Yelle, have you prayed about it? Have you sought God on it? What does His Word say about it?" He always gave the best advice. He was wise.

Earlier this year, something happened during church one Sunday that I haven't shared with anyone until now. It's been etched in my mind ever since and is something I think about all the time… especially now.

Every Sunday, Mom and Jeff sat about three rows ahead of me. This particular Sunday during worship, I watched Jeff. He had both his hands raised high, worshipping the Lord like he did every other Sunday. But for some reason, this Sunday, I couldn't take my eyes off of him. And for the entire song, I watched him, and as I watched him, I cried because at that moment, I had this overwhelming love fall on me for Jeff.

As I watched him, I felt so proud of him. I was so proud to have had him as my dad. I felt so blessed to have had such a Godly man to nurture me.

I never knew why that was such a profound moment for me. I never knew why I thought about it so often, but now just months later, I believe with all my heart that God gave me that memory of Jeff. I believe He gave me my own special memory that I get to keep and carry with me. Jeff led by example—He and Mom both have. And my goal in life is to lead my kids to Jesus the way that Jeff and Mom have led the boys and me.

I love you, Jeff, and thank you for loving me.

Jared's Eulogy

A lot of you knew him as Jeff Zbranek, but I was lucky enough to know him as Dad. The thing about my dad is he was a man with many great characteristics, so it's hard trying to summarize his life in just these few moments.

He was kind.

He was patient.

He was genuine, and every time I said, "I love you, Dad," he never failed to respond with "I love you too, Son." But the thing I love most about my dad is how humble he was.

Some of my earliest memories involve him finding me, no matter what I was doing, and apologizing. Regardless of what it was, if my dad felt in his heart that he was wrong about even the smallest thing, he would always make sure to apologize. My dad had a heart for people, and he wanted to make sure he treated everybody with love.

Looking back, there's no way I could have recalled what he did, but because he went out of his way to make things right with a small child, I will always remember how amazing my dad was.

I had heard the story he was once told, "Jeff, you're a good man." And my dad's response was, "the only good in me is Jesus." That shows just what kind of man my dad really was. He was a godly man who just wanted to be like Jesus.

I know my dad would have loved to have been here with us, but I also know that if this whole situation brings just one person to the Jesus that he loved so much, that would make him happy.

My dad knew where he stood in life and the Father, who he stood there with. And he would just want to make sure everybody got a chance to stand there with them. After my grandpa passed away, anytime the two of us were alone, he would smile and say, "My dad knows everything now."

It's hard for me to smile right now, but I can tell you one thing is certain, my dad knows everything now.

Joshua's Eulogy

My son, Josh, sent this text to me, which was read at his dad's funeral.

I'm not good at talking, so I'm gonna text it.

You said you wanted proof that God is real. The proof is all around you. The fact that you're alive and healthy is proof there's a God.

Dad once told me that he couldn't have kids and that he knows God healed him. Soon after ya'll had Jared. Jared and I are proof of God's existence. And the best proof you could ask for was Dad himself. There's no way you can be the kind of man he was without the Lord. It's impossible. And if God is real, then Heaven is real also, and Dad's there right now. He may not have received his healing here on earth, but he received his perfect healing in Heaven.

Romans 14:8 (ESV) says,

> *For if we live, we live to the Lord, and if we die, we*
> *die to the Lord. So then, whether we live or whether*
> *we die, we are the Lord's.*

And James 1:12 (ESV) says,

> *Blessed is the man who remains steadfast under trial,*
> *for when he has stood the test he will receive the crown*
> *of life, which God has promised to those who love him.*

God's Word says He heals and performs miracles, but that's all we ever focus on. His Word also says that there will be death and hard times. The only thing we can do is keep praising and thanking the Lord for the husband and father He gave us and the time we had with him.

I never got a chance to tell Dad my favorite scripture, but I'm going to tell you because it helps me. And I only found this scripture because you and Dad wanted to read the Bible with me every night. Matthew 28:20 (NIV) says,

> *And surely I am with you always, to the very end of*
> *the age.*

You're not alone and never will be. God is with you, Mom. I love you.

John's Tribute

I had asked my son-in-law (John), who is a songwriter/musician, to play a song at Jeff's funeral. He wanted to write an original song but said he wasn't able to come up with anything. He told me that he had given up, but something told him to go back and try again.

He said he prayed and asked the Lord to let him hear from Jeff or asked was Jeff okay and was he with Him (the Lord)? He picked up his guitar started playing, and all of a sudden, the words "I am not walking alone" came to him through God, and then the lyrics just started pouring out. He wrote this song in about thirty minutes, and he truly believes it is from the Lord. I hope that it will bless you as much as it has blessed and comforted me.

(The song can be found on Spotify under the artist's name—Johnathan Montague.)

REJOICE, REJOICE

by Johnathan Montague

I don't know if I told you
Just how beautiful life's been
I wouldn't change a single day
I would live it exactly the same again
I'm so sorry I had to leave you
I didn't mean to let you go
Just know where I've gone to now
Every step I take the streets are gold

I'm not walking alone
I am here in His arms embrace
No need to feel sorrow
Because I'm not walking alone

Now my life is a story
To be told now and then
I'm in the presence of His glory
With a love that never ends

I'm not walking alone
I am here in His arms embrace
No need to feel sorrow
I'm not walking alone

Rejoice, rejoice lift up your voices now
Rejoice, rejoice in the Lord
Rejoice, rejoice I'm with my Jesus now
Rejoice, rejoice in the Lord

August 20, 2021, at 10:11 AM — The Day My Life Changed Forever

We've all been there; we sympathize, we console, do a few acts of kindness, and then walk away. But today, for me, it's a different story. Before my loss, my life was good, and my faith had not yet been tested. Nothing can prepare you for the road you are about to walk.

Maybe, you are like me. You suffered the loss of a loved one, you're struggling with your faith, or just longing to feel God's presence. I long for God's presence as I walk through the unknown.

Not everyone will grieve the same. What helps me cope with loss may not work for someone else. There is no right way, or wrong way to grieve, although you will experience many different emotions. There is no particular order in which you will grieve, and the length of time will vary for each individual. I can tell you this, the greater we love, the greater the grief. Make sure that the things you are seeking for comfort are helping you and not hurting you.

I pray as I tell my story of walking through the fire, and being refined, that you will find a sense of peace and comfort that will help you in your journey from mourning to joy.

Revelation 21:4 (NIV) says, one day "…there will be no more death' or mourning or crying or pain…"

CHAPTER 1

Broken

Turn to me [LORD] and be gracious to me,
For I am alone and afflicted.
The troubles of my heart are multiplied;
Bring me out of my distresses.
Look upon my affliction and my trouble,
And forgive all my sins

—Psalm 25:16 (AMP)

What do you do when tragedy knocks on your door? It hits you in the stomach, knocking the wind out of you, and you can barely breathe. Your first thought is... *This can't be real things like this don't happen to me.*

As the minutes, hours, days, and weeks go by, my life seems as if it's spinning out of control. There's nowhere I can run or hide to escape the hurt and pain that has left me drowning in my own tears. My heart has been ripped out of my chest, leaving me empty and alone. I feel as if I have a heavy fist clenched in my chest, and that constant feeling remains as if it is now a part of me.

WAIT, it is a part of me now; it's a part of the new me. I liked the old me. I want to go back. I want everything to be like it used to be.

How did I end up on this journey?

Why was I chosen to walk this path?

Lord, do you hear me when I pray?

Are you still there?

Do you still love me?

Why am I here, in this nightmare that will never end?

Day after day, night after night, nowhere to run, nowhere to hide. And yet, life goes on for everyone else, as if nothing ever happened. Don't they know, doesn't anyone care that life has crushed me beyond repair. I can't be fixed. I will forever have a piece of me missing. What once was will never be.

None of this makes sense. I want to scream until I can't scream anymore. I want to tear all the memories off the wall, leaving them bare and empty like my soul.

This is exactly how I felt when I lost my husband to COVID on August 20, 2021. I didn't see it coming, I wasn't ready, and I definitely wasn't prepared for what lay ahead. One thing is for sure, it has turned my life upside down, and I am still trying to put the pieces of my life back together. But how can I fit all the pieces together when they are not all here?

Some of the pieces are missing. They don't fit anymore. I don't know what to do. I can't fix it. Oh God, help me. I am broken, but I'm Yours, take these broken pieces of my life, put me back together, and use me, Lord, in a great and mighty way to further Your kingdom. Not my will, but Your will be done, Lord.

CHAPTER 2

Denial

For though I fall,
I will rise again.
Though I sit in darkness,
The Lord will be my light.

—Micah 7:8 (NLT)

The Bible says that God has numbered our days. He is in control, and nothing happens without Him allowing it. God knows everything in advance, with His perfect omniscience. Before you or I was born, He had already determined the length of our days.

We can find peace in knowing that our loved ones are in Heaven and that one day we will see them again. Because this promise comes from God, does it mean that we won't hurt, feel pain, or experience loneliness? Absolutely not, the sorrow and grief... it's real, and the pain in my heart is unbearable. Sometimes I look in the mirror, and I wonder *Who are you, Will you ever be the person that you once were?*

As I write this, we are still experiencing the COVID-19 pandemic. Hundreds of thousands of people in the United States have lost their lives. Panic and fear have swept through our homes and communities. People have buried their husbands, wives, sons, daughters, mothers, fathers, grandparents, and friends without an explanation of who, what, where, or why this had to happen.

I received a call Friday morning, August 20, 2021, at approximately 8:30. "Mrs. Zbranek, your husband has taken a turn for the worse. You and your children need to get here as soon as you can."

The words were scrambled in my head. I am still trying to process what I just heard. As we rushed out of the house, I saw all the healing scriptures we had taped to the wall proclaiming Jeff's healing every day in the name of Jesus.

God, what happened?

I stared out the window as we drove to the hospital, looking toward the heavens, and all I could say was, "Not today Lord, not today Lord, please not today.

Jeff had been in the hospital for fifteen days, and not once were we allowed to see him, COVID protocol. He was so close and yet still so far away. I felt robbed and cheated of the last days that he was still alive, but today, this day, the last day we were allowed to see him.

We were dressed in protective gear from the top of our heads to the soles of our feet as we entered his room. My Jeff, just lying there so helpless. I was in total shock, numb, speechless. Is this really real?

My children were praying, but I couldn't take my eyes off of him. He begins to go into cardiac arrest, and the doctors and nurses scurry around the room as we continue to pray and believe for a miracle. "TOD (time of death) 10:11," she says. What! You're calling his death, that's it? Looking down without saying a word, she shook her head as she walked out of the room.

I am left standing there in a room of silence that once filled the air with sounds of beeping, alarms, and utter chaos. I walked over to him, put my arms around him, put my cheek to his cheek, and whispered in his ear, I love you. I kissed his forehead, I kissed his cheek, I kissed his hand, and I looked at the tear that had rolled out of his right eye.

They say that when you die, you rise above your body and witness everything that is going on with you at that moment. I do not know if that is true, but what I do know is this, that if it is true, then Jeff knows that he was not alone when he passed on to be with the

Lord. We were there with him, his children and I; we were there for his homecoming.

It's been said, dying is the easy part; it's the living that is hard. Oh how true this is.

Lord Your Word says in 2 Kings 20:5 (NKJV),

> *...I have heard your prayer, I have seen your tears; surely I will heal you.*

Lord, I have prayed many prayers, and I have cried many tears. I beg you to heal my shattered heart.

Once again, I stared out the window as we drove home, looking toward the heavens, this time not knowing what to say.

It is appointed to man, to live and to die (Hebrews 9:27).

> *Tomorrow is promised to no one.*
>
> — Walter Payton

> *And as it is appointed unto men once to die, but after this judgment.*
>
> — Hebrews 9:27 (KJV)

Did you know that God never intended for us to experience death here on earth? When Adam sinned, death came into the world. If Adam would never have sinned, then we would never have had to experience death. We would have lived forever.

> *"I have told you all this so that you may have peace in me. Here on earth you will have many trials and sorrows. But take heart, because I have overcome the world."*
>
> —John 16:33 (NLT)

CHAPTER 3

Anger

Though you have made me see troubles,
many and bitter,
you will restore my life again;
from the depths of the earth
you will again bring me up.
You will increase my honor
and comfort me once more.

—Psalm 71:20–21 (NIV)

Everyone was praying.

Didn't you hear us?

Didn't you know this was going to break my heart?

You took him anyway.

Didn't You care?

We had dreams.

We had plans.

We still had so much to do together.

You are a good God, so *why?*

I was raised in a Christian home and always believed in the Lord. So, what happened when death knocked on my door? I wish I could tell you that I stood strong in my faith, on a strong foundation during this storm and never wavered, but that's not the case.

If the truth is to be known, I was tossed to and fro in the storms of life, and I was doing my best to stay afloat. I just couldn't get to a place where I believed anymore. I didn't believe anything or anyone, and I questioned everything. Would you believe I asked God if He was real? I even asked if Heaven existed.

I wanted to know where Jeff was. I wanted to know if Heaven was real and if my Jeff was with Him and was he happy, or was he just lying in a box that we had buried him in. I kept telling the Lord if He would just let me know, it would help me in my healing process. I just needed to know, but nothing. I didn't hear anything from the Lord; He was silent.

I was mad, I was angry, but not necessarily at God. As I said, I was raised in a Christian home, and I have enough knowledge of God planted in me that every time I questioned God, in the very same breath, I would run to Him for comfort, guidance, and answers. I struggled with being double-minded, and it drove me crazy. I couldn't find the peace that I was so desperately searching for, I couldn't feel God's presence, and I couldn't hear Him speak to me.

God where are you? I am Your child, and You are my heavenly father. I am standing on Your Word, and I am standing on your promises. It's all that I have, but it's all that I need. Lord, please.

I know there is no way that you would bring people into our lives to love and then take them away never to see them again. Lord, Your Word says to give You thanks in the good times and to give You thanks in the bad times. I don't understand, how can I thank You… What do I say? Thank You Lord, for taking my husband and leaving me alone?

He was my husband, my companion, my friend, my love. I go to bed alone. I wake up alone. I face each day alone. I'm alone, Lord, I am alone, is all I could say.

The depth of this pain is piercing. It's the only way that I know how to describe it, and it won't go away.

And yet, even in the midst of my sorrow, God reminded me in Isaiah 53:5 (NIV), *"but He (Jesus) was pierced for our transgressions, He was crushed for our iniquities; the punishment that brought you peace was on Him, and by His wounds you are healed."*

(Emphasis is mine)

Thank you, Lord, for the mercy and grace that You show me each and every day, and thank you, Lord, for reminding me of what You did for me on the cross at Calvary. And forgive me, Lord, when I doubt Your Word.

...Lord I believe, help my unbelief.

—Mark 9:24 (NKJV)

CHAPTER 4

Bargaining

The Lord hears his people when they call to Him for help.
He rescues them from all their troubles.
The Lord is close to the broken hearted;
he rescues those whose spirits are crushed.
The righteous person faces many troubles,
but the Lord comes to the rescue each time.

—Psalm 34:17–19 (NLT)

I am not a perfect person. I don't have it altogether, but what I am, is a real person experiencing real hurt. All the masks that we put on to hide our hurt, pain, shame, or our failures have been removed... I am who I am...

Who Am I?

I am strong because I've experienced weakness.
I am healed because I've experienced pain.
I am whole because I've been broken.
I am beautiful, despite my scars and wounds.
I can laugh because I've experienced sadness.
I can live because I've been redeemed.
I am, who I am.
I am loved.

No matter what we do, God never stops loving us. Through this entire journey, I have questioned God, I have doubted God, and at times I didn't even believe God. In this lifetime, we will experience walking in the valley and on the mountain tops. For most of my life, I've experienced the mountain top, but now I walk through the deepest valley. The Bible says do not test God, but I found myself trying to bargain with God (Luke 4:12). If it doesn't fall under the same category, it has to be pretty close.

I remember praying one day when Jeff was in the hospital, and I told the Lord if He would bring my husband home to me, that I would spend the rest of my days telling His people about Him. I was making a deal with the Lord. I was telling Him of all the reasons why He couldn't take Jeff and why he needed to come home:

- The birth of Jeff's first biological grandbaby, Joel Luke Zbranek.
- Jeff's promise to the boys that he was going to buy the boat they always talked about.
- To attend our youngest son's engagement/wedding.
- Our plans of building a new home.
- Our plans of traveling.
- Our plans of just seeing our children and grand-children growing up.

Jeff did not receive his healing here on earth, but I know he is in Heaven with the Lord. I also know that the Lord knows everything and that He will always do what is best for His children, even when we don't understand.

Good people pass away; the godly often die before their time. But no one seems to care or wonder why. No one seems to understand that God is protecting them from

evil to come. For those who follow godly paths will rest
in peace when they die.

As you already know, my faith was surely shaken through all this, and this is exactly where the enemy wanted me, doubting the Jesus that I have always known. Even though Jeff did not come home to me here on this earth, I will continue with the promise I made to the Lord, and I will continue to tell people about the Lord and His goodness.

CHAPTER 5

Depression

This is my comfort, my consolation
My breath of fresh air
In the midst of my depression and loss
Your Word nourishes and repairs me
It revives my life
Your promises restore me, and
Makes me whole.

—Psalm 119:50
(Paraphrased, Adrianna Robinson)

Death is cruel. It's so final. The last chapter of a person's life here on earth. The voices, the footsteps, the laughter that once filled our lives and home is gone. There's a quietness to my soul that I can't explain. Sometimes I wonder will I ever laugh again, will I ever be the same.

After Jeff's passing, I began looking to the sky for signs. I would fall on my knees and beg God for answers. The Lord says He will never give you more than you can handle (1 Corinthians 10:13). I'm not sure I quite understand how He measures our tolerance level. My mother-in-law Ruby passed away on July 11, 2021, from lung cancer. My husband Jeff passed away on August 20, 2021, from COVID. My aunt Pat passed away on August 28, 2021, from COVID, which was also the day after we buried Jeff, and my aunt's daughter Patsy passed away on October 18, 2021, from COVID. This alone was too much for my family and me to bear, and if this is not a recipe for depression, then I don't know what is.

My daughter would come to visit me every Saturday just to comfort me and help out in any way that she could. She surprised me one day and showed up on a Sunday only to find me outside crying on the phone. She told me, "Mom, I think it's time that you start taking your pills."

Did I mention yet that the doctor had prescribed me pills for depression? They were prescribed to me right after Jeff passed. I had put them on the window sill in the kitchen, and that is where they sat for weeks—months. I would look at the bottle every day, but I did not want to take them. I've always been healthy, never taking any kind of medication other than for a cold or an antibiotic here and there when needed. I was scared to take the pills that were prescribed to me because I didn't know how they were going to alter my behavior. I didn't want to walk around like a zombie, nor did I want them to suppress my feelings.

There is healing in our grief when we cry, and I have to say that I always feel a little better after each breakdown. It releases the stress that, if it's held in, makes you feel like you are going to explode internally.

So, I took my daughter's advice, and I started taking the medicine that Sunday night before I went to bed. When I woke up the next morning, I felt nauseous and shaky. I told her how I felt, and she said, "Mom, sometimes you have to take them for a while to get the medication into your system."

I reluctantly took another pill before I went to bed the next night and felt the same way Tuesday morning when I woke up, nauseous and shaky. I didn't think too much about it, other than that I needed to take this prescription for a few more days to get it into my system, and then things would start to level out for me, so I thought. But wait, that evening around six, I told my son, "I am going to go take a shower." He was standing in the kitchen cooking and said, "Okay." I walked down the hallway and took one step into my room.

Before I go any further, let me ask you this question: do you know that God speaks to you? He speaks to our hearts. Did you know that Satan speaks to you? He speaks to our mind (battlefield of the mind), and just as God has a plan for your life, Satan also has a plan for your life as well. Satan is always on the prowl seeking whom he can devour. Scripture says that he comes to kill, steal, and destroy our lives (John 10:10). And yes, he even attacks during our tragedies when we are at our weakest and most vulnerable.

Back to my story, I stepped into my room and these thoughts immediately came to my mind: *You don't belong.*

I stood there for a minute and thought, *Where did that come from?* At that moment, I had an overwhelming sense of sadness that flooded my soul, and I began to cry uncontrollably. I went into the bathroom, sat down, and just cried with all these thoughts whirling around in my head… *you're alone, he's never coming back, you will never be the same, why wasn't he healed, everyone else's lives are still good,* and on and on and on the thoughts kept coming.

I knew that I had to get control of these thoughts because I knew they weren't from God. I knew I needed prayer, and I needed it *now.* It's a good thing when your brother is your pastor; I have prayer 24/7.

I walked through the house headed toward the back door, and my son said, "I thought you were taking a shower."

"Not now," I told him. "I need prayer."

I called my pastor and told him what happened, and he told me this, "The enemy wants nothing more than to take you out and destroy the rest of your family." He prayed for me and said, "Stay strong, Trish. We are all praying for you."

My son had walked outside to check on me, and at that moment, he had overheard me telling my pastor what had happened in my room. He turned around and went back inside without saying a word. When I was through praying with my pastor, I headed back inside. I heard someone talking as I opened the back door and asked if someone was here. He said no, and at that moment, I knew exactly what he had done. He went into my room and began casting out evil spirits that had no place being in my room, in our house, much less in our lives.

I am so proud of my children that they know and serve the Lord. Children learn what they live, and my children know that they have the authority in Jesus' name to cast out demons, to pray over the sick, to speak in new tongues, and to pull down strongholds.

Jeff always prayed over our children, he prayed over me and prayed over our house. Jeff loved the Lord, and he left his handprints all over our lives. Jeff is not in my past; he is in my future, and I long for the day to see him again.

As for me and my house, we will serve the Lord.

— Joshua 24:15 (KJV)

Needless to say, when I had gone back into my house, I researched the medicine that I was taking, and one of the side effects was thoughts of suicide.

When you lose a loved one, and the grief is so sharp, sometimes the thought crosses your mind that you don't want to live anymore. It doesn't mean that you are suicidal, but I do want you to know that it can be part of the grieving process. Maybe not for everyone, but it was for me.

I no longer take the pills, even though I know that there is a certain amount of pain and hurt that I must endure, I will trust the Lord to carry me through.

Trust God with your wounds.

CHAPTER 6

Acceptance

To everything there is a season (...)
A time to be born, and
A time to die (...)
A time to heal
A time to break down, and
A time to build up;
A time to weep, and
A time to laugh;
A time to mourn, and
A time to dance;

— Ecclesiastes 3:1–4 (KJV)

The last time I checked, the sun still rises, the sun still sets, and the clock keeps ticking. I have no choice but to get up every day and keep breathing because time stands still for no one. If only we could turn back time to the day when everything was okay.

But even if He doesn't...

In the Book of Daniel, it tells the story of three men, Shadrach, Meshach, and Abednego. They had a firm foundation in their faith and their commitment to God. King Nebuchadnezzar had built a towering gold statue and ordered everyone to bow down and worship the statue, and anyone who refused would be thrown into the fiery furnace. When Shadrach, Meshach, and Abednego refused to worship the statue, they replied to the king:

If that is the case, our God whom we serve is able
to deliver us from the burning fiery furnace, and
He will deliver us from your hand, O king.

—Daniel 3:17–18 (NKJV)

Even if my God didn't answer our prayers and heal Jeff, the way
we wanted Him to, we will still serve our God.

Broken to Blessed

At the moment, I am four months into my journey, and I think about Jeff every day. I learned in my Grief Share class that people can get stuck in their grief, and it's not a healthy place to be when grieving. Not only is this unhealthy for you, but it is also unhealthy for your loved ones around you. So, we must be careful where we keep our minds and our thoughts that we ponder. You don't want to stay in those thoughts too long, as they can bring feelings of depression over you.

Everyone heals at different phases in their journey of grief, and as I know, others will reach a healing point sooner than I. What I have found that helps me is to keep my mind busy. I read a lot just searching for answers or trying to connect with someone else's feelings. I like to write. I have written in a journal since the day that Jeff became sick, and that is what has inspired me to write this book.

I have even taken up a new hobby. My son-in-law is teaching me to play Jeff's acoustic guitar. Who knows, maybe I will end up writing a song one day. I am at a time in my life where I am trying to adjust to a new lifestyle. All my responsibilities have been cut more than in half, and I have more time than I know what to do with.

I am, willingly or not, learning to accept the fact that Jeff is gone. The days are long, the weekends are longer, and some days are tougher than others. God help me through this as I am struggling.

Someone once told me exercise is good for the soul, and it is. Sometimes I feel like the walls are closing in around me, so it's nice to get out and feel the sun on my face, fill my lungs with fresh air, and just look at nature's beauty.

A friend of the family asked this question, speaking of Jeff. "Do you think God took one soldier home so that he could save many soldiers?" Because Jeff's passing made such an impact on the lives of many, similar statements like this have been said more than once. When I think about it, a part of me says I could see this as part of

God's plan. I am not saying this is what God did, but I know Jeff, and I knew his heart and how much he loved the Lord. Genesis 50:20, I have heard this scripture more times than I can count, but it had always been paraphrased, "what the enemy meant for evil, God will turn it for good."

It wasn't until after Jeff passed that I looked this scripture up and read its entirety. Genesis 50:20 (NIV) says, "You intended to harm me, but God intended it for good to accomplish what is now being done, the saving of many lives." And the statements that were made actually did make sense. God could have taken Jeff home to save others. We do not know the mind of God or His plans for our lives. We just have to trust Him even when things do not make sense.

But the other side of me, the broken side of me, says, why did I have to sacrifice my husband for others to be saved? To truly live for God, one's attitude must be, no matter the cost, I will give a sacrifice. When you make the decision to walk with God and to follow Him, it will require sacrifice and perseverance from you. Did you know that God accomplishes more through our pain than He does through our success? What would you say if I asked you what has Christianity cost you?

To be honest, until now, it hadn't cost me anything.

Lucky is the spouse who dies first,
Who never has to know what survivors endure.

— Sue Grafton

A friend of mine sent me this quote on December 31, 2021, which was also Jeff and I's anniversary. The holidays were very hard for me this year, and I just couldn't wait for them to be over. Maybe, like me, you were struggling to find joy in Christmas this year.

Christmas was our favorite time of the year. I loved to decorate our home while Jeff searched on finding the perfect gift for everyone. But this year… the hustle and bustle of the holidays, just like my life, had come to a screeching halt. I felt paralyzed, and all I could do was go through the motions. What once held significant meaning just doesn't mean that much to me anymore. It was hard. I did my best to smile on the outside while feeling crushed from every side on the inside. Everything seemed so surreal to me again at that moment, as if the bandage on my wound had been ripped off once more, leaving everything exposed.

When you lose a loved one, it changes you. It changed me. I look at the world around me, and I look at the people in it, and I see them through new eyes. Lord, let me see Your people through Your eyes and the way that You see them. I have been given a greater sense of compassion for God's people, before I only sympathized, but now I share their pain.

In the midst of my suffering, I find comfort in comforting others. I know that I am not walking this road alone, and even if it takes me all day long to take one step forward, I will keep pressing on, giving God all the glory even when I don't understand. God shows His strength in our weakness.

> *"Where, O death, is your victory?*
> *Where, O death, is your sting?"*
>
> —1 Corinthians 15:55 (NIV)

Death has the power to put Christians in the grave, but when death is defeated, Christians will rise out of their graves and be set free for eternity. Death paralyzes our soul, but after it is destroyed, it will no longer have this power, and Christians will fear death no more.

You can stand on this promise.

God, you are still good.

God, you are still faithful.

God, you love me.

> *"...that all things work together for good to them that love God."*
>
> — Romans 8:28 (KJV)

Anyone who has experienced loss knows the difficult path to recovery, and if my story can give you the strength to get out of bed each morning, the courage to face unimaginable agony, or the resilience to keep taking one step at a time, down a path where there seems to be no light then I have accomplished what God has called me to do.

> *He comforts us in all our troubles, so that we can comfort others. When they are troubled, we will be able to give them the same comfort God has given us.*
>
> — 2 Corinthians 1:4 (NLT)

My heart in writing this book was to share my experience walking through this season of pain, brokenness, and struggles.

> *When you pass through the waters, I will be with you; and through the rivers, they shall not overflow you. When you walk through the fire, you shall not be burned, nor shall the flame scorch you.*
>
> — Isaiah 43:2 (KJV)

Maybe you feel like you are holding your life in charred remains, but God doesn't call us to walk through the fire to be burned. We walk through the fire so that He can rebuild us into the person that He has called us to be.

Thank you, Lord, for turning my ashes into beauty (Isaiah 61:3).

Like it or not, you are on the right path. You are on the path God has called you to walk one day at a time, even when we don't understand. Trust God with your healing, trust God with your future, and trust God with your life.

CHAPTER 7

Blessed

*He will wipe away every tear from their eyes, and
death shall be no more. neither shall there be mourning
nor crying, nor pain anymore for the former things
have passed away.*

— Revelation 21:4 (RSV)

God's message of hope to a lost and hurting world.

The last chapter of this book belongs to the Lord. As I was writing the first six chapters, I told the Lord, the last chapter belongs to You, and I will not write anything until You tell me what to write.

Ever since Jeff's passing, I have been praying and asking God to show me Heaven and to show me Jeff, that he is there with Him, and that he is happy. Then I wouldn't feel so guilty about still being here, being able to enjoy our children and life without him.

I told the Lord I knew this would help me in my healing process,. I even asked Him to take me on a personal tour of Heaven in a dream. That may sound odd to some of you, but that is the kind of relationship that I want with my God, I want to be able to ask Him anything, and that is the kind of relationship that He desires to have with His people.

Of course, this is what I thought the Lord would reveal to me, a glimpse of Heaven, and then have me write about it so that I could share it with everyone. After Jeff's passing, I had an obsession with learning as much as I could about Heaven.

Did you ever realize that the Bible doesn't teach a lot about Heaven, but what it does teach us is what we need to do and how we should live our lives to make it to Heaven. All I talked about was going to Heaven, to see Jeff. I would tell my son, "I just want to see your dad again." He told me, "Mom, your thinking is all wrong." He said, "You should want to go to Heaven to see Jesus first, and then you will see Dad." I was stunned by his reply, I was in my own pity party, and I thought that everyone should feel sorry for me as well. But then reality hit, and I told him "Yes, you are right, Son." My children are of much wisdom, just like their father, and during this difficult time, they are pulling from the well that has been planted in them over the years.

> *Train up a child in the way he should go: and when he*
> *is old, he will not depart from it.*

> — Proverbs 22:6 (KJV)

I repented and asked the Lord to forgive me for putting Jeff before Him. The Bible says that we are not to put anyone or anything before God. Scripture says that our God is a jealous God, and He will not share His glory (Exodus 34:14. Let's take a look at the Ten Commandments, the first two:

- *"You shall have no other Gods before me"* (Exodus 20:3 NKJV). There is only one God we worship, the creator of all things and to whom we live for.
- *"You must not make for yourself an idol of any kind or an image of anything in the heavens or on the earth or in the sea"* (Exodus 20:4 NLT). We make idols out of so many things in our lives. Anyone or anything that you put before God or takes time away from God is an idol. It's funny how we think we have

everything figured out. We think we know the plans of God and how He is going to work things out according to our plans.

My plans aren't your plans, nor are your ways my ways, says the Lord. Just as the heavens are higher than the earth, so are my ways higher than your ways and my plans than your plans.

— Isaiah 55:8–9 (CEB)

But God… He had different plans on what He wanted me to share with you.

On December 29, 2021, I went for a walk, talking to the Lord. *I am almost finished writing my book. What do You want me to tell Your people, Lord?*

On December 30, 2021, early that morning, I had a dream, and in that dream, Jeff gave me a scripture.

Make them holy by your truth; teach them your word, which is truth.

— John 17:17 (NLT)

I know and believe with all my heart that this scripture is the message the Lord wants me to share with His people. After all, there is nothing more important than sharing God's Word with the world. After all, if you don't know the Word, you don't know God, and if you don't know God, you will not spend eternity with Him.

If you haven't made the connection yet, let me expound on it for you. The Lord had Jeff bring me the scripture, which was the message that He wanted me to share with you, and that was how to prepare for Heaven.

I didn't see Jeff in Heaven as I had asked, but I know that the Lord, in His timing, will not only give me the tour of Heaven I asked for but that He will also show me Jeff there with Him as well. I bring my request to the Lord daily.

> *Listen to my voice in the morning, Lord. Each morn-*
> *ing I bring my requests to you and wait expectantly.*

> — Psalm 5:3 (NLT)

The Lord also tells me that He will show me great and mighty things. It's all in Scripture, and what He promises to do for me, He will also do for you.

> *"Call to Me, and I will answer you, and show you*
> *great and mighty things, which you do not know.*

> — Jeremiah 33:3 (NKJV)

Our God is a God who cannot lie. He is the same yesterday, today, and forever. Stand on the Word of God and all the promises which He has promised you.

As I reflected on my thoughts when I just knew that I knew the Lord was going to reveal Heaven to me so that I could share His glory and majesty with you. *What a glorious finale that would be as an end to this book,* so I thought.

But as I pondered on what the Lord did reveal to me what He wanted me to show you, it made perfect sense; of course, it would, He is God. Let me break it down for you. Why would God want me to tell you about Heaven and its beauty that awaits us as our eternal home if some of you may not even know how to get there. Isn't that just like God, to keep things in proper perspective? Let's learn what God expects of us first, apply it to our lives, and wait expectantly for the return of our Lord Jesus Christ.

If you're like me, you've heard the Lord is coming back soon, probably more times than you can count. I am not perfect, I am only human, so I am going to tell you what I think. I have heard this for as long as I can remember, and it still hasn't happened. What happens when we hear something over and over, and it does not come to pass?

We hear it, but it takes no root in our lives. We do not heed to it, so we put it on the back burner "per say". But I will tell you this, as I examine the world we live in today, with all the evil unfolding around us, witnessing the signs of the end times that we are taught in the Bible, I know without a doubt the Lord's return is soon. 2 Peter 3:9 (NIV) tells us this,

> *The Lord is not slow in keeping His promise, as some understand slowness. Instead He is patient with you, not wanting anyone to perish, but everyone to come to repentance.*

So, what is He telling us in this scripture exactly? God is saying this. No one should go to hell. God is being patient in His return, giving everyone the chance to repent and to know Him intimately. He does not want anyone to perish, and what does the Bible say about this? My people perish "for lack of knowledge" (Hosea 4:6 KJV). God desires that *all* people be saved and come to know the knowledge of the Word of God.

Matthew 28:19 (NIV), Jesus instructs us to "go and make disciples of all nations…" We have to be bold and unashamed. As disciples, we are to teach others the truth.

> *For whosoever shall be ashamed of me and of my words, of him shall the Son of man be ashamed…*
>
> — Luke 9:26 (KJV)

In the next few pages, I am giving you the opportunity to accept the Lord as your savior. To be born again and to be confident that your name is written in the Lambs Book of Life. You see, it's not about me or you. It's never been about me or you. It's about the one we serve.

Today is the day to get your life's priorities in line.

- J — Jesus
- O — Others
- Y — Yourself

And then you will have joy in your life. Because He died and gave His life for me, I gave my life to Him.

Salvation

Deny yourself, take up your cross, and follow me.

— Matthew 16:24

As a Christian, we are to be the hands, feet, and voice of Jesus. We are to win the souls of the lost. I am not asking you to believe what I believe, but I am asking you to believe in the Lord God Almighty.

In this life, nothing else matters if you don't end up spending eternity with our Lord Jesus Christ. The Bible clearly tells us in John 3:3 (NIV),

"...no one can see the kingdom of God unless they are born again."

If you knew a thief was roaming around your neighborhood, would you sleep with your doors open, or would you stay awake and be ready?

"Behold, I am coming like a thief! Blessed is the one who stays awake..."

— Revelation 16:15 (ESV)

We live in a fallen world, a nation, a world that has turned its back on God. In a day when people are calling good evil and evil good, in a day when people mock the Word of God.

If my people, who are called by name will humble themselves, and pray and seek My face, and turn from

their wicked ways, then I will hear from heaven, and I
will forgive their sin and will heal their land.

— 2 Chronicles 7:14 (NKJV)

How do we get to this place of repentance and asking God to be Lord of our lives?

For many, it isn't until tragedy strikes, or maybe you've hit rock bottom financially, experienced broken families/relationships, gone through a divorce, received a bad report from the doctor, or suffered the loss of a loved one. It is during these times that life brings us to our knees... What do you do, where do you go, or where do you turn?

All God wants is your heart and to have a close personal relationship with you. Our God is a good God. He is faithful and just. He doesn't make it hard to enter into His Kingdom. All He asks of us is to turn from our wicked ways, invite the Lord to live in your heart, and love the Lord your God with all your heart, soul, mind, strength, and to love your neighbor as yourself. It's that easy!

The Bible teaches that God has a day prepared when He will judge *all* men. If we are going to be judged by God's Word, then we must also live by God's Word.

Are you ready for the judgment day?

The first thing you need to do to ensure where you will spend eternity is say the sinner's prayer with true repentance in your heart, and I would like to give you that opportunity today.

Sinners Prayer

Dear Lord Jesus, I know that I am a sinner, and I ask
for your forgiveness. I believe you died for my sins and

rose from the dead. I turn from my sins and invite you
to come into my heart and life. I want to trust and
follow you as my Lord and Savior.[1]

If you said that prayer and meant it from your heart, welcome to the Kingdom of God. Find a Bible believing church, and know that your Heavenly Father is rejoicing with your decision to follow Him.

…unless a kernel of wheat falls to the ground and dies,
it remains only a single seed. But if it dies, it produces
many seeds.

— John 12:24 (NIV)

This scripture reminds me of Jeff. He was a single seed, but when he died, he produced many seeds.

No matter the cost Lord, you have my sacrifice.

1   Billy Graham Evangelistic Association, "My Peace with God., Billy Graham, 2022.,https://lp.billygraham.org/my-peace-with-god/?msclkid=c74a33d4b10f11ec8d8e2e03ecdc69a3.

MY WALK WITH CHRIST

I gave my life to the Lord in May of 1995. I remember the day and exactly where I was. I was on the floor, on my knees in my living room, when I surrendered my life, when I prayed and asked the Lord to come live in my heart, to be my Lord and Savior. I remember the love that I felt immediately for others and the excitement of being a new creation in Christ.

> *Therefore, if anyone is in Christ, the new creation has come; The old has gone, the new is here!*
>
> — 2 Corinthians 5:17 (NIV)

What does this mean? It means that we want to remove the things in our lives that are not pleasing to God and that is contrary to His Word. And yes, God even brought to my remembrance people that I had unforgiveness towards in my heart. Right then, He gave me love and compassion for them, and I had an overwhelming urgency just to call them and ask for their forgiveness. It was like a weight being lifted from my shoulders. When we carry unforgiveness towards others, we are actually the ones who are held captive.

> *For if you forgive other people when they sin against you, your heavenly Father will also forgive you. But if you do not forgive others their sins, your Father will not forgive your sins.*
>
> — Matthew 6:14–15 (NIV)

Our first promise in forgiving is eternal life.

Heaven isn't for good people, heaven is for forgiven people.

—Greg Laurie

Over time the cares of this world and just the busyness of life began to distract and take my attention away from the Lord. It became more of a one-sided relationship, with Jesus always being there for me but being more of a convenience for me.

Are you aware of the story in the Bible about Martha and Mary (Luke 10:38–42)? Let me paraphrase to give you the idea. Martha opens her home to Jesus and His disciples as they are traveling. Martha is busy cooking, serving, and waiting on Jesus, while her sister Mary sits at the feet of Jesus listening to Him speak while doing nothing to help Martha in preparations for their guest. Martha becomes upset and says to the Lord, "'Lord, do you not care that my sister' is not helping me?" (Luke 10:40 BSB), and Jesus replies, "'Martha, Martha, you are worried' and distracted 'by many things,'" but few things are needed (Luke 10:41 BSB). "'Mary has chosen' what is better, 'and it will not be taken away from her'" (Luke 10:42 BSB).

I guess you could say I became a Martha, in fact, some of my family members used to call me Martha because of the busyness that my life reflected. You see, the enemy will bring things in our lives to distract us from serving our God. The enemy knows you, and he knows me; he knows our weaknesses, and he knows just what buttons to push. This is why it is very important for us to pray and stay strong in the Word. I am sad that it took the loss of my husband to open my eyes, to slow me down, and to reprioritize my life.

But today… I eat, I sleep, I breathe the name of Jesus. I wasn't always like this, but now when I wake up, He is the first thing on my mind. All throughout the day, He is on my mind. When I go to bed,

He is the last thing on my mind, and when I wake up throughout the night, He is always on my mind.

When you go through a storm, if you put your trust in Jesus, you'll never come out the same. The Lord is the anchor of my soul.

It was a day like any other when my storm began, but now it's a day like none other. My relationship and love for God have only deepened through this crisis, and I have to tell you again, God doesn't make mistakes. I may not understand what He is doing in my life right now, but I was born for such a time as this.

> *"For if you remain silent at this time, relief and deliverance for the Jews will arise from another place, but you and your father's family will perish. And who knows but that you have come to your royal position for such a time as this?"*
>
> — Esther 4:14 (NIV)

God has given each of us a purpose and the opportunity to further His kingdom. God didn't place you or me in a position where we should be consumed only of ourselves, but He has positioned us in a world where every day it is a battlefield, and for some, we may be their first and only line of defense.

Wouldn't it be tragic if we missed an opportunity to serve the kingdom of God because we were focused only on our kingdom?

How many souls could be saved if we would just step up to the call that God has on our lives?

> God isn't looking for perfect people, He is looking to perfect people.
>
> —John Hileman

I want you to know that today I love the Lord, with all my heart, with all my soul, with all my mind, and with all my strength.

If you don't love the Lord like this, tell Him, He already knows, and guess what He's not mad at you. Tell Him, Lord, I don't love You the way You desire Your people to love You. I need You to show me how to love You, and He will.

God is a good God. Let's all get ready for that *big* family reunion in the sky.

SERMONS

I would like to include a few sermon videos from pastors that I have found very helpful. These sermons had really helped me and comforted me when I was going through the really dark days of my life. Some days I would listen to these sermons over and over just to keep feeding my spirit with the Word.

Free Chapel Church, Gainesville Georgia

- Pastor Jentzen Franklin — *Where Is God*
- Pastor Jentzen Franklin — *God Uses Life's Bruises*

Gateway Church, Southlake Texas

- Pastor Robert Morris — *Death*
- Pastor Robert Morris — *The Beginning of Death*

Fresh Life Church, Kalispell Montana

- Pastor Levi Lusko — Book and Sermon Series

Through the Eyes of a Lion
- Jennie Lusko — Book *The Fight to Flourish*

...It is written, Man shall not live by bread alone, but by every word that proceedeth out of the mouth of God.

— Matthew 4:4 (KJV)

DONATIONS

*Will a man rob God? Yet ye have robbed me. But
ye say, Wherein have we robbed thee? In tithes and
offerings.*

— Malachi 3:8 (KJV)

Have you ever asked yourself this question… What does God want
me to do for Him while here on this earth? We were all created for
a purpose, to be the hands, feet, and voice of Jesus.

*"'For I was hungry and you gave me something to eat,
I was thirsty and you gave me something to drink, I
was a stranger and you invited me in, I needed clothes
and you clothed me, I was sick and you looked after
me, I was in prison and you came to visit me.' Then
the righteous will answer Him, 'Lord, when did we
see you hungry and feed you, or thirsty and give you
something to drink? When did we see you a stranger
and invite you in, or needing clothes and clothe you?
When did we see you sick or in prison and go to visit
you?' The King will reply 'Truly I tell you, whatever
you did for the least of my brothers and sisters, you did
it for me.'"*

— Matthew 25:35–40 (NIV)

*If you are struggling with the question, what does God
want me to do, let me suggest that you could start out
by helping those that are less fortunate, and the King*

will reply to you, "Whatever you did for the least of my
brothers and sisters, you did it for me."

— Matthew 25:40 (NIV)

God loves a cheerful giver. Jeff was a cheerful giver, and I have listed missions that were near and dear to his heart.

Life Outreach International
Water for Life — Life Today with James Robison
PO Box 982000
Fort Worth, Texas 76182–8000
1–800–947–5433

International Fellowship of Christians and Jews
PO Box 97339
Washington, DC 20077–7472
800–249–9003

"I will bless those who bless you..."

— Genesis 12:3 (NIV)

Day Star Television
'Heart for the World'
PO Box 612066
Dallas, Texas 75261–2066
www.daystar.com
817–571–1229

First State Bank
Jeffrey Zbranek Memorial Scholarship (Offered to students in Matagorda County only)
PO Box 457
Blessing, Texas 77419
361–588–7777

A memorial scholarship in Jeff's memory has been opened to continue sowing seeds into the lives of God's children.
Make a difference in someone's life today.

Whoever is kind to the poor lends to the Lord, and He will reward them for what they have done.

— Proverbs 19:17 (NIV)

SUICIDAL

Satan, the enemy, is the father of all lies. He looks for a lie to fill your mind, and he makes you believe this lie about yourself and believe that there is no reason for your existence. He wants nothing more than to convince you that you're alone and that there is no hope.

I have the mind of Christ.

— 1 Corinthians 2:16 (NIV)

I was speaking with a friend one day, and she shared a story with me about a man she knew who had lost his wife, and within that same year, he committed suicide. The grief was too much. The pain had a death-grip hold on his heart.

Not everyone knows how to handle grief. In fact, do any of us know how to handle grief? We're not given a manual that says what to do, when to do it, and how to do it. I didn't want to live anymore. I wasn't suicidal, but just the thought of having to live my life without Jeff was too much to process. I felt as if I had no purpose in life anymore. But because I had such a loving and caring support system, I did not go down the suicidal path, but I very easily could have.

It's like that fork in the road, you reach the end, and you have to make a decision. Do I go left, or do I go right? One way will lead you to life, and the other way will lead you to destruction.

There are hurting people everywhere; they are all around us. Do you want to be more like Jesus? Care about His people; let Him love a lost and hurting world through you. If you ever find yourself or know someone in overwhelming grief that you can't escape, I encourage you to seek professional counseling immediately.

Help is available. Call this number today.

1–800–273–8255
National Suicide Prevention Lifeline
Hours: Available 24 hours
Language: English and Spanish

The three-digit code 988 has been designated and will route all callers to the National Suicide Prevention Lifeline. Some areas may currently be able to connect to the lifeline by dialing 988. This dialing code will be available to every area across the United States beginning July 16, 2022.

Don't give up the fight. Find yourself in His healing arms today, and let your pain be washed away by His love. Even in our grief and sorrow, God is with us.

PRAYER

Life has been difficult for so many that I would like to take this time and pray for each of you. God's Word tells us to bear one another's burden, to pray for those that are lost, hurting and broken.

Let us pray...

Heavenly Father, I come before you on this very day with a humble spirit and a grateful heart on behalf of all your children. I lift up each individual to You, Lord, You know who they are, and You know them by name. Lord, You know the hurt and the pain that each of us carries. We surrender our lives to You and lay it all at the foot of the cross. Lord, it is too much for us to carry this burden alone. You have seen every tear that we have cried, and You have felt the loneliness in our hearts. Your Word says that You are our healer, You are our comforter, and that You will never leave us nor forsake us. Lord, we can't do this on our own. We cannot walk this road alone. We need You, Lord, and I ask that You will wrap Your loving arms around each of us today, let us feel Your presence, and let us know that You are near. Open our eyes, Lord, that we may see the promises that You have for us, and open our ears that we may hear when You speak to us. Give us a heart like yours, O God, that we may love as You have loved us. I ask that You will lead us, guide us, and direct us in the plans that You have for our lives.

In the name of Jesus, we pray, Amen.

MY WORDS OF ENCOURAGEMENT TO YOU

Sometimes people come into your life for a moment, a day, or a lifetime. It matters not the time they spent with you, but how they impacted your life in that time.

— Anonymous

Everyone's progression through loss, while always devastating, will always be different, and I want to thank you for walking through my journey of loss with me. I hope in some way it's helped you, helped to bring you clarity, or just made a bit of difference in your life. It's hard to imagine that anything great could ever come out of life's hardships, but God sees our tomorrow, and God has a bigger plan for our lives than we have for ourselves.

I don't know what God has planned for my life, much less what He has planned for your life, but what I do know is that if we can truly believe what God's Word says about our lives, then it can bring us hope where there seems to be no hope. And I know that God's plan for our lives is far better than any plans that we could ever have or even imagine. You see, we are not defined by our brokenness, but we are defined through the love that God has given us and through the love that we give to others.

Lord, show me how to love the unlovable.

How we treat others during our time here on earth determines the kind of legacy that we will leave behind and whether or not we are remembered or forgotten. But no matter what type of legacy you leave behind, God knows everything about you, whether good or bad, and He still loves you most. I want you to know that I love you and that I am praying for everyone around the world who is suffering from a broken heart. There is no distance in prayer. When we can't hold hands in the physical, we can connect hearts in the spiritual.

I want to leave you with this.

When everything seems to be at its darkest, I want you to know that there is light in your future. Maybe you want to know if I've seen the light. Not yet, but I have seen glimpses of the light, and it's what gives me the hope that I need to keep moving forward. I know that I am getting stronger each day. Things that I could not do before, I can now do without feeling like I am going to suffocate.

I am still walking out my healing process. I still cry most days, and my heart is still heavy, but some days are better than others, and some days the sun shines just a little brighter. I want to tell you, please don't give up. Accept the Word for what it is, and the Lord for who He is. Surround yourself with people who love you, that will encourage you, lift you up, and can help you through this journey because you will need them.

Maybe you want to tell me that you don't have anyone, that you are all alone. If this is you, I encourage you to reach out to a local pastor in your area. I know that he will lead you in the right direction. That's why we are here, to be the hands, feet, and voice of Jesus, to help one another out in times of trouble. Like my husband, I have a heart after God's own heart, and I have a heart for God's people. Pour out your pain and troubles to the Lord, and let Him love on you today.

> "...Love the Lord your God with all your heart and
> with all your soul and with all your mind. This is the

first and greatest commandment. And the second is like
it: 'Love your neighbor as yourself.'"

— Matthew 22:34–39 (NIV)

If God be for us, who can be against us?

— Romans 8:31 (KJV)

Know that I love you,
But mostly know that God loves you,

broken_blessed@yahoo.com

I love you, Jeff
I miss you, and
I will see you again one day.

REFERENCES

Amanda. 2015. "Thoughts." Only Time. 2015. https://tenshiamarie. blogspot.com/.

Billy Graham Evangelistic Association. 2022. "My Peace with God." Billy Graham. 2022. https://lp.billygraham.org/ my-peace-with-god/?msclkid=c74a33d4b10f11ec8d8e2e03ec-dc69a3.

"Quote by Anonymous." 2022. SearchQuotes. 2022. https://www. searchquotes.com/quotation/Sometimes_people_come_into_ your_life_for_a_moment%2C_a_day%2C_or_a_lifetime._It_ matters_not_the_time_the/454848/.

"Quote by Greg Laurie." 2018. Harvest.Org. 2018. https://harvest. org/resources/gregs-blog/post/heaven-isnt-for-good-people/.

"Quote by John Hileman:" 2022. Goodreads, Inc. 2022. https:// www.goodreads.com/quotes/420168-god-isn-t-looking-for-perfect-people-he-is-looking-to.

"Quote by Paul Shane Spear." 2018. Quotation Celebration. 2018. https://quotationcelebration.wordpress.com/2018/10/01/ as-one-person-i-cannot-change-the-world-but-i-can-change-the-world-of-one-person-paul-shane-spear/.

"Quote by Walter Payton." 2022. Brainy Quote. 2022. https://www. brainyquote.com/quotes/walter_payton_335879.

ABOUT THE AUTHOR

A small-town girl with a Texas-size heart. I have been taught about God and His goodness from little up. God was preparing me for the journey that I would walk in this lifetime. I lost my sister in a tragic car accident when she was sixteen years old, which was the first trial I remember our family having to face. But God… He pulled us through.

I myself was in a motorcycle accident at the very same age, sixteen, and my parents were told that I would not survive. But God… He pulled me through. He wasn't finished with me, He had a plan and a purpose for my life.

Then there was the loss of my husband, another trial to face, but God… He is pulling me through because, again, He is not finished with me yet. I know that God has always had a call on my life, a call to serve, a servant's heart. For a season in our lives, my husband and I fostered children.

> *As one person I cannot change the world, but I can*
> *change the world of one person.*
>
> —Paul Shane Spear

My heart then and now is to love God, love His people, and tell as many about Him as I can. God brings people into our lives every day, be the reason they smile, be the reason they know Christ, be the reason that Heaven is their eternal home.

CPSIA information can be obtained
at www.ICGtesting.com
Printed in the USA
LVHW010524210622
721699LV00013B/390